DIGITAL CITIZENS

RIGHTS AND RULES

By Ben Hubbard

Illustrated by Diego Vaisberg

W
FRANKLIN WATTS
LONDON • SYDNEY

Franklin Watts
First published in Great Britain in 2018 by
The Watts Publishing Group
Copyright © The Watts Publishing
Group 2018

Credits
Series Editor: Julia Bird
Illustrator: Diego Vaisberg
Packaged by: Collaborate

ISBN 978 1 4451 5812 9

Franklin Watts
An imprint of
Hachette Children's Group
Part of The Watts Publishing Group
Carmelite House
50 Victoria Embankment
London EC4Y 0DZ

An Hachette UK Company
www.hachette.co.uk
www.franklinwatts.co.uk

Printed in China

MIX
Paper from
responsible sources
FSC® C104740
FSC
www.fsc.org

CONTENTS

WHAT IS DIGITAL CITIZENSHIP?

When we log onto the internet we become part of a giant, online world.

In this world we can use our smartphones, tablets and computers to explore, create and communicate with billions of different people. Together, these people make up a global digital community. That is why they are known as digital citizens. When you use the internet you are a digital citizen too. So what does this mean?

CITIZEN VS DIGITAL CITIZEN

A good citizen is someone who behaves well, looks after themselves and others, and tries to make their community a better place. A good digital citizen acts exactly the same way. However, the online world is bigger than just a local neighbourhood, city or country. It spans the whole world and crosses every kind of border. It is therefore up to all digital citizens everywhere to make this digital community a safe, fun and exciting place for everyone.

RULES ARE BORING:
WHY DO WE HAVE
THEM?

OFTEN THEY ARE THERE
TO PROTECT YOU.

IS IT MY RIGHT TO
BAN MY BROTHER
FROM USING MY
TABLET?

UMM...

MY DIGITAL RIGHTS AND RULES

Citizens that behave well and follow the rules of their
community have certain rights. A right is something a
person is entitled to as a human being, such as food,
shelter or protection from harm. Rights also give people
certain privileges, such as free speech. This book is all
about your online rights, as well as some rules you should
follow to be a good digital citizen.

KNOW YOUR RIGHTS

In today's world, everyone should have the right to become a digital citizen with access to the internet.

As digital citizens, we also have certain rights when we go online. But to keep these rights we need to behave responsibly and play by the rules. So what are a digital citizen's rights, rules and responsibilities?

RULES

Sometimes it can seem like the internet has no rules. But it actually has many of the same rules as the real world. For example, it is against the rules to bully others or tell lies about them. It is also against the rules to steal other people's work, or download things illegally (see pages 22-23). Your school or parents may have some of their own rules about how you use the internet too.

SARAH SAYS YOU POSTED A RUDE COMMENT ABOUT HER SHOES.

RESPONSIBILITIES

Being a responsible digital citizen means behaving in the same way you would in the real world. That means respecting others, being polite, protecting yourself and people you know and helping others when you can.

RIGHTS

Just like in the real world, you have the right to be safe, protected and free from abuse while online. You also have the right to privacy, free speech and the right to look freely for information. However, access to some websites may be against the rules of your school, parents or country.

RULE OF THE TOOLS

For many people, having a digital device that is constantly connected to the internet seems like a normal part of everyday life.

But we should never take these for granted and remember that they are tools, not toys. For this reason, it's important to take care of your digital devices and use them responsibly. This means switching them off in places you're not supposed to use them.

PHONE HOME

Your parents may have some rules about when you can use your phone, tablet or computer and for how long. It doesn't always feel like it, but these rules are often there for your own good. It's also fair that your parents set these rules. After all, they are usually the ones paying for you to be online!

SCHOOL RULES

Your school may also have rules about when you can use your digital device. Often they are in place so you pay attention in class and don't disrupt others. Good digital citizens respect the rules and use their common sense about using their digital devices outside of the classroom too. Talking loudly or playing music on smartphones is not a good way to behave in libraries or on public transport.

DEVICE WATCH

With so much of our personal information on our smartphones, it pays to take extra care of them. Most of all, this means never leaving them unattended in public. After all, a phone is an easy thing to snatch.

INFORMATION INVASION

The internet is a free resource and we should all have the freedom to seek and receive information from it.

However, sometimes websites that are harmful or inappropriate for children are blocked. You can ask a teacher or parent to explain why you have been blocked from using certain websites. Digital citizens should be allowed to ask about online rules so they can understand why they are obeying them.

WHY CAN'T I OPEN THE NASA WEBSITE TODAY?

AND I CAN'T VISIT NATIONAL GEOGRAPHIC ANYMORE!

FILTERS

Internet filters are put in place to block websites with particular content, such as sex or violence. These websites aren't good for children and can be confusing or upsetting. However, sometimes filters also block helpful websites by mistake. If you think something has been blocked incorrectly, point it out to a parent or teacher.

WHICH WEBSITES ARE HARMFUL?

Websites that are definitely harmful are those which promote hatred or violence towards others. Websites with adult themes such as sex or violence are also not appropriate for children. Websites that ask for your personal information should always be avoided. However, a simple rule of thumb is: if you see anything that you don't like on a website, just click out.

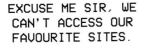

EXCUSE ME SIR, WE CAN'T ACCESS OUR FAVOURITE SITES.

OUR NEW CONTENT FILTERS MUST HAVE BLOCKED THEM BY ACCIDENT. I'LL GET THIS FIXED.

FREE SPEECH

Free speech is one of any citizen's central rights, including digital citizens.

This means not being scared to say what you think when you post a comment, message or blog online. However, it doesn't mean being able to say anything at all. In the online world people need to respect others and their opinions, even if they disagree with them.

WHAT IS FREE SPEECH?

Free speech is a recognised human right according to international law. It gives people the right to express themselves without interference. This important right was partly won during the 18th century French and American revolutions, when people rose up against their rulers.

FREE SPEECH GONE BAD

Freedom of speech is not covered by law when people say rude or hurtful things about others. This is especially true when attacks are made against people because of their skin colour, sexuality, religion or country of origin. These are known as hate crimes and are taken very seriously by the police.

RESPECTING OPINIONS

The online world is a free place where people should give their opinions openly and respect the right of others to have different opinions. As long as they are not hurting others, different opinions are what make both the real and online worlds such interesting places.

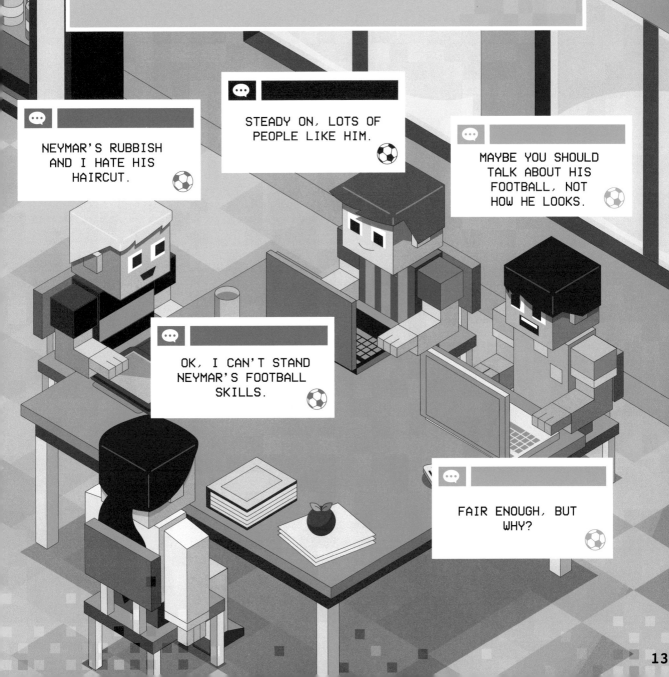

PROTECTING OTHERS, PROTECTING YOURSELF

In the online world we have to look after ourselves and the people around us.

That means protecting them from things that could be harmful or upsetting. It's easy to share or write things on social media, or post photos to our accounts. But if not checked first, these can sometimes have consequences later on.

PERSONAL INFORMATION

Your personal information is made up of your private details: your age, name, school, telephone number and address. These are things you need to protect when you are online, so strangers can't find out too much about you. You need to protect the details of your friends and family too.

REVEALING PHOTOS

Have you ever heard the saying 'One picture is worth a thousand words?' This can be true of photos you post online. Often these can give away too much personal information about yourself or your friends — such as where they live or go to school. Make sure to check a photo before you post it.

LOOK, THE PHOTO SHOWS HENRY'S HOUSE NUMBER AND STREET NAME.

YOU'RE RIGHT, IT'S GIVING TOO MUCH OF HENRY'S INFORMATION AWAY. I'LL TAKE A DIFFERENT SHOT.

HURTFUL COMMENTS

Good digital citizens report and delete nasty messages, emails or texts and never spread them around. If someone has said something hurtful about someone you know online, it's your responsibility not to forward it on.

PRIVACY PARTICULARS

Many of us use social media accounts to keep in touch with friends and family.

When we post information such as photos or blogs we assume it will stay only on the social media website. But how can we be sure? Sometimes we might find our posts and photos appearing elsewhere on the internet.

I LOOK SO GROWN-UP, I CAN'T WAIT FOR EVERYONE TO SEE MY PHOTO.

PRIVACY POLICY

Every social media website has its own rules about how your information is used. It is up to you to check you are happy with a website's privacy policy and that your information will be protected from being shown elsewhere. The easiest way is to ask a trusted adult to help you read a social media site's privacy policy before joining it.

SOCIAL SETTINGS

The privacy settings on your social media account allow you to choose who looks at what you post. Choosing 'only friends' is the best setting. You can often also adjust the settings so only a selected group of your friends can see your photos, posts or other most private information.

LOOK, MY PHOTO IS ALL OVER THE PLACE, I DIDN'T AGREE TO THIS.

I THINK YOU'VE FORGOTTEN TO SET THE CORRECT PRIVACY SETTINGS ON YOUR SOCIAL MEDIA ACCOUNT.

INFORMATION ASTRAY

Making sure our information is protected on our social media accounts is important. But once we post something online we no longer have complete control over it. Photos are easy to copy and post elsewhere and there is always a risk your account will be hacked. This is why it's important to be happy with the things you post.

DIGITAL LAW

Digital law is designed to protect digital citizens against online crime.

Online crime can include identity theft, illegal downloading and bullying. However, every country has different laws about online crime and there is no international police force looking after the internet. That is why if you see something you think is harmful or wrong, it is always a good idea to report it to a trusted adult.

HARASSMENT AND BULLYING

While many countries agree that online bullying is a crime, not all agree on what should be done about it. When online bullying happens among children, often the local police work in conjunction with the school. Those found guilty can be expelled from the school or prosecuted under harassment laws. The simplest thing is to tell a trusted adult if it is happening to you or someone you know.

EWWW! SOMEONE HAS PUT HORRIBLE PICTURES ALL OVER MY WALL.

COME ON, LET'S TELL MY DAD.

WHAT ARE ONLINE CRIMES?

The following are typical online crimes:

1 Hacking into websites

2 Stealing someone's information or identity

3 Illegal file sharing

DEFAMATION

Telling lies about someone is a crime known as defamation. Defamation can be something that is written, known as libel, or something that is spoken, known as slander. Defamation is very serious if somebody tells lies that damage a person's reputation. If someone is found guilty of this crime, they often have to pay a lot of money to the person they defamed.

THANKS FOR SHOWING ME. I'M GOING TO CONTACT YOUR SCHOOL AND THEN THE POLICE.

4 Plagiarising people's work (see pages 20—21)

5 Creating viruses

6 Pirating software

ORIGINAL ONLINE WORK

Can you imagine if you wrote an essay, article or book that somebody then claimed was their work?

This is what it is like for people who have their work plagiarised. Under copyright law, it is illegal to pretend to have created something that you have not. This includes using someone else's writing for school essays and homework.

> JULIE, I NEED TO SEE YOU ABOUT YOUR ASSIGNMENT.

CITING SOURCES

Often when we are doing research we find a writer has summed up something so well that we wish we had written it ourselves. It's okay to use a writer's exact words if you get permission to do so and then attribute the text to them. This is called 'citing your sources'. You can ask your teacher how to cite sources in your homework and essays.

ESSAYS AND HOMEWORK

It's easy to cut and paste a sentence from a webpage and then drop it into your own essay or homework assignment. It may not seem serious, but doing so is plagiarising someone else's work. In serious cases, students have handed in whole essays that they have copied directly from the internet. It's not difficult to find out if something has been plagiarised and it can get that person into a lot of trouble.

I REALLY LIKED YOUR ESSAY, BUT THERE WERE SOME SENTENCES THAT YOU PASTED STRAIGHT FROM THE INTERNET.

I THOUGHT ONE SENTENCE HERE AND THERE WAS OK.

IT WOULD BE IF YOU ATTRIBUTED THE SENTENCES TO THE ORIGINAL AUTHOR. LET ME SHOW YOU HOW TO DO THAT.

ILLEGAL DOWNLOADS

It might seem like lots of people download music, films and games for free these days.

However, downloading any material that is under copyright is stealing and is therefore against the law. Copyright law applies to everyone, no matter what age they are. That means anyone that illegally downloads files could get into trouble.

WHAT IS COPYRIGHT?

When somebody creates something, such as a book, song or films they own it under copyright. This means they get to decide what happens to it. To use the work, people normally have to seek the copyright-holder's permission and pay a fee. This stops people stealing the work of others. It also means if you download something which is under copyright for free, you are breaking the law.

ILLEGAL DOWNLOADING

There are many legal websites where you can pay a fee to download films, songs or books. Then there are other illegal websites that offer these files for free. By using these sites, people are not only breaking the law but also run the risk of downloading a file that contains harmful malware or viruses. Often the quality of these files can also be very poor. It is best to avoid these websites and file-sharing altogether, even if it is tempting to get something for nothing.

I DOWNLOADED THAT MOVIE, BUT THE SOUND IS RUBBISH.

PHEW! GLAD I DIDN'T JOIN IN.

AND MY LAPTOP STARTED ACTING WEIRDLY AFTERWARDS.

YEAH, ME TOO. I'M SORRY.

ACCESS FOR ALL

Today, digital technology is all around us.

We use this technology to learn, have fun and message our friends. Surely everyone in the world must own at least one digital device, such as a laptop, tablet or smartphone — right? That's not actually the case. In many places, children don't own any digital devices. Others don't have access to the internet at all.

YOUR TURN IN 15 MINUTES.

A WORLD OF OPPORTUNITY

Good digital citizens believe that everyone should have online access, regardless of who they are, where they live and how much money they have. No one should miss out on the amazing opportunities the online world can offer.

HOW CAN I HELP?

There are lots of ways you can help bring internet access to those without it, both in your own community and beyond. Here are a few of them:

RECYCLE OLD DEVICES

Ask your teacher if your school can set up a recycling box for old, unwanted digital devices. These phones, tablets and computers can go to less fortunate people in your area, or abroad.

FUNDRAISERS FOR FACILITIES

Holding a fundraiser, such as a bake sale, can help your school buy digital devices for your school library or computer room, or to lend out to pupils. Ask your teacher about organising one.

DID YOU KNOW ONLY AROUND HALF THE PEOPLE ON EARTH HAVE INTERNET ACCESS?

BAKE SALE TODAY

FOR SALE

DID YOU KNOW ONLY AROUND 30 PER CENT OF PEOPLE ON EARTH OWN A SMARTPHONE?

ASK YOUR PARENTS

Adults can be helpful sometimes because they know lots of other adults. Ask your parents if they know any businesses that would donate money or digital devices to your school. They might be happy to help when they find out what you're doing.

HELP EVERYONE PARTICIPATE

Helping others participate in the online world can often begin close to home.

There are always people around us who don't have the latest phone or tablet. There are many others who can't use their digital devices properly! Good digital citizens try to involve and educate those around them, so everybody can keep up with the latest trends and technologies.

INCLUDING EVERYONE

It's easy for those without a digital device or internet connection to feel left out. But you can include them by showing them the latest applications on yours. After all, we all need help learning new things from time to time.

COME AND HAVE A LOOK AT HOW THIS NEW MESSAGING APP WORKS.

SPECIAL NEEDS

Some pupils with special needs can struggle using digital devices. They may not be able to see them well or find it hard to hold them. Schools should always make sure these pupils are getting the same access as everyone else. If you see they are not, talk to your teacher about helping them.

THIS IS HOW YOU
SEND A MESSAGE.

HOW DO YOU INVITE
MATES TO JOIN?

DIGITAL DIVIDE

The Digital Divide refers to the gap between those who have digital access and those who don't. With the spread of smartphones, more people have access to the internet than ever before. But there is still a long way to go before everyone can be a digital citizen.

DIGITAL QUIZ

Now you've reached the end of this book how do you feel about your digital rights and rules?

How much have you learned? And how much can you remember? Take this quiz and tally up your score at the end to find out.

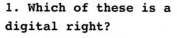

1. Which of these is a digital right?
a. To be given a free smartphone
b. Freedom of speech
c. Freedom to say anything to anyone

2. The gap between those who do and do not have internet access is called:
a. The Internet Interval
b. The Online Opening
c. The Digital Divide

3. Where should you not use your smartphone?
a. At the beach
b. In class
c. At the park

4. When is it OK to use an author's work from online?
a. When you cite your sources
b. When you change all the letters into capitals
c. By taking out all the apostrophes

5. What privacy setting should you use on your social media account?
a. Only my friends
b. Friends of friends
c. Everyone

6. Which of these is a form of defamation?
a. Tribal
b. Libel
c. Mabel

7. Which of these is not an example of your personal information?

a. Your avatar
b. Your real name
c. Your address

8. Which of these is not an online crime?

a. Hacking into websites
b. Calling someone stupid in a blog
c. Stealing someone's identity

HOW DID YOU DO? ADD UP YOUR SCORE TO SEE.

1-4: You are on your way but retake the quiz to get a score over 4.

5-7: You've passed the quiz well. Now see if you can pass the quiz in the book *My Digital Future.*

8: Wow! 8 out of 8. You are a natural born digital citizen

ANSWERS

1: b; 2: c; 3: b; 4: a; 5: a; 6: b; 7: a; 8: b

GLOSSARY

Avatar
A computer icon or image that people use to represent themselves online.

Block
A way of stopping someone from sending you nasty messages, or being stopped from entering a website.

Digital
Technology that involves computers.

Download
To take information or files from the internet and store them on your computer.

Hack
To break into computers and computer networks online.

Internet
The vast electronic network that allows billions of computers from around the world to connect to each other.

Malware
A dangerous computer programme that is created to damage or disable other digital devices.

Online
Being connected to the internet via a computer or digital device.

Privacy settings
Controls on social media websites that allow you to decide who has access to your profile and posts.

Search engine
A computer programme that carries out a search of available information on the internet based on the words you type in.

Sexuality
A person's sexual feelings, whether they are attracted to a person of a different sex or the same sex.

Smartphone
A mobile phone that is capable of connecting to the internet.

Social media
Websites that allow users to share content and information online.

Trusted adult
An adult you know well and trust who can help you with all issues relating to the internet.

Virus
A dangerous program that can 'infect' a computer, destroying the information it holds.

Website
A collection of web pages that is stored on a computer and made available to people over the internet.

HELPFUL WEBSITES

Digital Citizenship
The following websites have helpful information about digital citizenship for young people:

http://www.digizen.org/kids/

http://www.digitalcitizenship.nsw.edu.au/Prim_Splash/

http://www.cyberwise.org/digital-citizenship-games

http://www.digitalcitizenship.net/Nine_Elements.html

Bullying
These websites have excellent advice for kids who are experiencing bullying online. There are also some free helplines, which children can call anonymously to receive expert help:

https://www.childline.org.uk/info-advice/bullying-abuse-safety/types-bullying/online-bullying
Childline helpline for kids:
0800 1111

http://www.bullying.co.uk
BullyingUK helpline for kids:
0808 800 2222

https://www.stopbullying.gov/kids/facts/

https://www.commonsensemedia.org/videos/cyberbullying-prevention-guide-for-kids

Staying Safe
These websites are dedicated to keeping kids safe online, with lots of good advice:

http://www.childnet.com/young-people/primary

http://www.kidsmart.org.uk

http://www.safetynetkids.org.uk/personal-safety/staying-safe-online/

http://www.bbc.co.uk/newsround/13910067

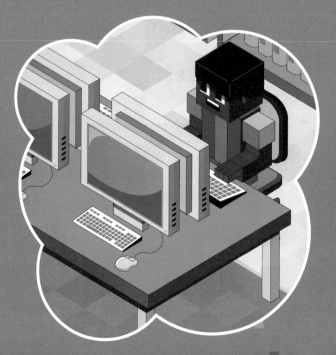

INDEX

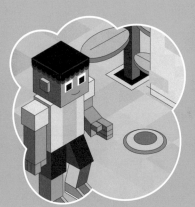

Health & Wellness

- What is digital citizenship?
- Your digital health and wellness
- Prepare to prevent pain
- Stretch, don't strain
- Digital training
- App attack
- Online time limits
- Online addiction
- Social media and self-image
- Avoiding adverts
- Being boys and girls
- Digital detox
- Digital quiz

Rights & Rules

- What is digital citizenship?
- Know your rights
- Rule of the tools
- Information invasion
- Free speech
- Protecting others, protecting yourself
- Privacy particulars
- Digital law
- Original online work
- Illegal downloads
- Access for all
- Help everyone participate
- Digital quiz

My Digital World

- What is digital citizenship?
- Connect, collect and communicate
- A world of websites
- Cyber searching
- Digital friendships
- To share or not to share?
- Messaging aware
- Phone etiquette
- Cyberbullying
- Bystanding
- Send a cyber smile
- A world outside
- Digital quiz

My Digital Future

- What is digital citizenship?
- Future technology today
- Dating digital devices
- The latest thing
- Digital maintenance
- Explaining the world
- Online shopping
- Technology in business
- Technology in schools
- Educating the world
- Technology tomorrow
- The future is unwritten
- Digital quiz

My Digital Community and Media

- What is digital citizenship?
- Social society
- My networks
- Gaming groups
- Hobbies and interests
- Netiquette
- Kindness, not cruelty
- Online news
- Spot the fake
- I am a brand
- Uniting online
- Shrinking the world
- Digital quiz

My Digital Safety and Security

- What is digital citizenship?
- Prepare to protect
- Trusted help
- Protecting personal details
- Passwords and Passcodes
- Cyberbullies and trolls
- Private social media
- Cyber strangers
- I'm in trouble
- Cyber criminals
- Pop-ups and pitfalls
- Viruses and malware
- Digital quiz